Celebrate and Remember Reconciliation

Home Guide

The publishing team included Gloria Shahin, editorial director; Joanna Dailey, development editor; prepress and manufacturing coordinated by the production departments of Saint Mary's Press.

Copyright © 2011 by Saint Mary's Press, Christian Brothers Publications, 702 Terrace Heights, Winona, MN 55987-1320, www.smp.org. All rights reserved. No part of this book may be reproduced by any means without the written permission of the publisher.

Printed in the United States of America

2327

ISBN 978-1-59982-072-9

Celebrate and Remember
Reconciliation

Home Guide

David Galusha

saint mary's press

Contents

Introduction 5

Chapter 1
In the Name of the Father, and of the Son, and of the Holy Spirit 13

Chapter 2
Trust in God's Mercy 17

Chapter 3
We Follow God's Word 21

Chapter 4
I Confess 25

Chapter 5
I Am Sorry 29

Chapter 6
Pardon and Peace 33

Chapter 7
His Mercy Endures Forever 37

Chapter 8
Go in Peace 41

Acknowledgments 45

Introduction
Welcome!

Your child's relationship with the Catholic Church began in the Sacrament of Baptism. At that time you brought your child to the entrance of the church, where you declared your willingness to bring her up within the Christian community and according to the Catholic faith. Now your family is ready to take the next steps in including your child in the life of the Church.

The next steps in the initiation of children into the life of the Church are the celebration of the Sacraments of Reconciliation and the Eucharist.

Just as you and your family took part in a preparation program prior to celebrating your child's Baptism, now you are asked to help your child to better understand the meaning of the Sacraments of Reconciliation and the Eucharist. In this period immediately preceding the reception of the Sacraments, it is vital that children receive more in-depth catechesis in the parish and in the home.

The *Celebrate and Remember: Reconciliation* Home Guide has been especially developed to assist you to use the child's book in formal at-home preparation for the Sacrament of Reconciliation. You have chosen to be the primary catechist in the process of Sacrament preparation, which is in keeping with your ongoing role in the religious formation of your children. Your pastor and parish catechists stand ready to offer you support and any assistance you feel that you need over the next several weeks.

Much of the informal preparation for Reconciliation has been ongoing in your home and in the parish community. Your child is already aware of your Christian moral values and the care with which you make moral decisions each day. Through your living of gospel values, the sense of moral responsibility has gradually come to be internalized within the family. Through your involvement with your parish community and in the celebration of the Eucharist, your child has undoubtedly come to view the Church as an instrument of forgiveness, consolation, and reconciliation.

Your prayerful and sincere dedication to this preparation for the Sacraments of Reconciliation and the Eucharist will provide an opportunity to strengthen your appreciation of your own faith, and then to share that faith with your child.

Before You Begin: Some Things to Consider

Preparing your child for First Reconciliation is a wonderful opportunity. You already know that how you present an activity can make a difference in your child's response. You, and your entire family, can help set the tone of Sacrament preparation. If you create this as a fun, meaningful, quality time with your child, he or she will likely come to look forward to this time together with you and will cherish the memory of it later in life.

Choose the time and setting for your First Reconciliation lessons carefully. Find a time and place that is relatively quiet, and minimize distractions by turning off the radio, television, and phones. Select a time when your child is not typically tired or hungry, or include a snack as part of the experience. By being attentive to such scheduling issues, you will make this a time together that everyone looks forward to.

Many families will complete each lesson in one sitting. However, if your child has a shorter attention span, or if it is a better fit with your family time, divide the lesson into several shorter meetings, or complete the lesson on Sunday and do the family activities on other days of the week.

When you are working with your child, take the time to listen. Don't give in to the temptation to rush your child to respond or to supply the answers yourself. Your interest and patience show your child that what he or she thinks is important to you.

In general, complete the activities alongside your child. For example, if your child is drawing a picture showing forgiveness, draw your own picture to share with your child. Be sure to keep extra paper handy for yourself.

As you become familiar with the home guide and the structure of the child's book, you will be more comfortable tailoring a lesson to be most effective for your individual child.

The Learning Process

The *Celebrate and Remember: Reconciliation* Child's Book is designed to help young children to understand forgiveness of sin and participation in the Rite of Penance. It is the basis for the other *Celebrate and Remember: Reconciliation* components.

The child's book consists of eight chapters that have ten pages each. Each chapter begins with a ritual prayer experience. This ritual prayer allows the learners to ground the chapter content in an experience of prayer that is directly related to the liturgy and the prayers and essential understandings associated with each part of the liturgy. The core content is then developed in We Listen, We Learn, and We Live. The chapter ends with a closing prayer in the We Pray section.

We Listen is a two-page section featuring Scripture that is tied to the focus of the lesson.

We Learn is a four-page section that presents the doctrinal and liturgical points of the lesson.

We Live is a two-page section that applies the lesson to your child's life.

We Pray is a one-page concluding prayer related to the content within the chapter. Your family can pray together for growth in faith and for strength to live as disciples of Christ.

The chart below illustrates how each chapter is constructed.

Page 1	Opening Prayer
Pages 2 and 3	We Listen (Scripture)
Pages 4 through 7	We Learn (Doctrine)
Pages 8 and 9	We Live (Application)
Page 10	We Pray (Closing Prayer)

Each lesson offers additional learning features in the child's book, which may include the following:

With My Family This feature appears three times in each chapter and provides quick and simple activities that you can do together as a family.

Faith Highlights This feature highlights points of Catholic doctrine your child should be familiar with as part of their preparation for the Sacrament.

Saint Spotlight This feature offers short biographies of saints. It familiarizes your child with other people of faith who can be examples for us.

Living Our Faith This feature provides specific teachings of the Church that have an impact on our daily lives.

In addition to the core chapters, the child's book also includes a resource section with the following special features:

Where We Celebrate Reconciliation This section illustrates the interior of a reconciliation room and describes a confessional, both used for individual celebration of the Sacrament.

The Sacrament of Reconciliation: The Communal Celebration This is an instructional outline of the liturgical rite of the Sacrament celebrated in community with the opportunity for individual confession.

The Sacrament of Reconciliation: The Individual Celebration This is a step-by-step outline of the Rite of Reconciliation.

An Examination of Conscience This feature provides an examination of conscience developed for young children to guide them as they prepare to receive the Sacrament.

Catholic Prayers and Practices This section contains some key prayers, including: the Sign of the Cross, the Lord's Prayer, the Glory Be to the Father, the Hail Mary, the Apostles' Creed, an Act of Contrition, and an Act of Hope, as well as listings of the Ten Commandments, the Beatitudes, the Precepts of the Church, and the teachings of Jesus.

Glossary This is a compiled list of terms and definitions that are helpful for those who are preparing for the Sacrament of Reconciliation.

Certificate Each child's book contains a frame-ready certificate that can be signed and used to mark the date of first reception of the Sacrament of Penance and Reconciliation.

Child's Book Contents

Chapter Title	Scripture	Key Church Teaching
1. In the Name of the Father, and of the Son, and of the Holy Spirit	God Forgives Us (Genesis 2:7-9,15-17; 3:1-24)	Baptism washes away sin and gives us new life. Jesus gives us the Sacrament of Reconciliation to bring us back to God when we sin.
2. Trust in God's Mercy	The Forgiving Father (Luke 15:11-24)	The Sacrament of Reconciliation is a gift of God's life that makes us new again.
3. We Follow God's Word	God Tells Us How to Live (Exodus 19:20, 20:1-17)	Jesus came to show us how to follow God's rules.
4. I Confess	Prepare Your Life for the Lord! (Matthew 3:1-6,13-17)	The Sacrament of Reconciliation is a sacrament of *conversion*.
5. I Am Sorry	Jesus Forgives the Sorrowful Sinner (Luke 7:36-40,47-50)	Sorrow for sin includes a resolve not to sin again.
6. Pardon and Peace	Jesus Brings Salvation (Luke 19:1-9)	In the Sacrament of Reconciliation, we are reconciled with God and all his people, the Church.
7. His Mercy Endures Forever	Jesus Is the Good Shepherd (Luke 15:1-7)	Jesus loves us even when we sin, and rejoices when we come back to him.
8. Go in Peace	Jesus Gives Us Peace (John 14:23-27)	The Sacrament of Reconciliation helps us to live as disciples of Jesus.

Liturgy	Prayer	Living Reconciliation
The priest welcomes us.	• The Sign of the Cross • We Praise the Trinity	We are called to be followers of Jesus.
The priest prays that we trust God's mercy.	• A Prayer for God's Mercy • A Prayer for Forgiveness	When we make bad choices, God is ready to forgive us in the Sacrament of Reconciliation.
We listen to God's Word.	• We Pray with the Word of God • We Pray to Follow God's Word	Jesus teaches us the New Commandment of love.
We confess our sins.	• Return to the Lord • The Lord's Prayer	The Holy Spirit gives us courage.
The priest gives us a penance.	• An Act of Contrition • The Hail Mary Prayer	We try to make up for our sins.
The priest gives us absolution.	• A Song of Peace • We Pray to Jesus	We have to work for peace.
With the priest, we thank God for his mercy.	• Praise for God's Mercy • Prayer to the Good Shepherd	Jesus never stops loving us.
We go in peace, because we are freed from our sins.	• Jesus Blesses Us • We Are Easter People!	We walk with Jesus along the "Conversion Road."

Understanding the *Celebrate and Remember: Reconciliation* Home Guide

This home guide is designed to help you prepare your child for First Reconciliation. Take time to get comfortable with it before you begin the lessons. Browse through it and look through the first lesson outline along with the child's book. This guide was designed with an easy-to-use format that will make the learning process simple yet effective.

Parent Background

The first page of every chapter begins with some basic background information for you. This information offers you deeper insight into the content of the chapter and provides you with reflection material that can help you prepare to teach your child.

GET READY!

The Get Ready! section points out any specific points of consideration or reflection that might enrich your teaching experience of a particular chapter. In addition to the specific directions in the Get Ready! section, it is helpful at this point to remember to read over the lesson and look at the pictures and illustrations presented throughout the child's book. Make notes about anything that strikes you at this time.

You will also want to read through the family activities and the additional activities that are suggested. Based on your time frame, decide which activities to incorporate into the immediate lesson and which to use throughout the week.

A prereading of the Heart to Heart section will also be helpful at this preparation stage. If you take this message and shape it into a real heart-to-heart talk with your child, it will become a rich, meaningful part of the lesson. The heart to heart talk is the part of the lesson when you can close the book and have a heartfelt talk with your child. Great learning can come from a real, honest sharing between you and your child.

GET SET!

The Get Set! section alerts you to any specific materials that you will need for the lesson. In addition to any items that might be mentioned, it is a good idea to create a container of materials that you will use regularly—pencils, erasers, crayons or markers, paper, highlighters, sticky notes, index cards, tape, scissors, a glue stick, stickers, a lighter or matches, and a family Bible or child's Bible. Keep these supplies, your child's book, and your home guide in a place that is convenient to where you will be teaching the lessons.

You will also want to set up a prayer space at this time. If you are working at your dining room table, make a centerpiece with a cloth, candle, cross or crucifix, and Bible. If you are gathering in your family room, set up your prayer space on a coffee table or bookshelf. Keep this space simple and uncluttered. It will be a special part of your prayer together.

Finally, as a step after all other preparation has taken place, the Get Set! section will offer a prayer that you can pray in preparation for the lesson ahead. Use the words provided, or create a spontaneous prayer to the Holy Spirit, asking for guidance and wisdom as you teach the lessons to your child.

GO!

You are now ready to begin. The Go! section gives you the first instructions of the lesson, which revolve around reading and discussing the chapter title and praying the opening prayer together.

Using Children's Literature as a Supplemental Resource

Picture books and short stories are a fun way to supplement the material in the child's book. Such resources often contain situations or themes that lend themselves to discussions about faith. The most important consideration is the main message of a particular book and whether that message can be directly correlated to a concept your child is learning in the Sacrament preparation process. If the message is abstract or is only partially related, it is best not to utilize that book with your child.

Keep in mind that there are probably a number of books with which your child is familiar that teach a lesson about responsibility, forgiveness, and reconciliation. Recalling these books is a first step to introducing new literature, since your child has spent some time considering the meanings of the stories. As an example, Beatrix Potter's *Peter Rabbit* would be too juvenile for you to read to a seven-year-old, but recalling it would spark a discussion of responsibility, repentance, forgiveness, and reconciliation. Look through your child's library for similar stories you can discuss together. You may find the following books helpful when preparing for First Reconciliation.

Children's Literature

1. *Red, Blue, and Yellow Yarn: A Tale of Forgiveness,* Miriam R. Kosman (Hachai Publishing, 1996). Donny finds his grandmother's red, blue, and yellow yarn lying on the bed. While he is playing with it, the yarn gets tangled up and Donny's mother is displeased. Helping him clean up the mess, Grandma tells a story about a similar mistake when she was a child.

2. *Show Each Other Forgiveness,* Just Like Jesus Said series, Melody Carlson (Broadman and Holman Publishers, 2002). A young boy has a frustrating day when nothing happens the way he intends. In the end, he learns forgiveness.

3. *Living the 10 Commandments for Children,* Rosemarie Gortler and Donna Piscitelli (Our Sunday Visitor, 2007). Parents will appreciate this book, which has been written for readers on two levels: Scripture for adults and stories for the children help the Commandments come alive.

4. *Beatitudes for Children,* Rosemarie Gortler and Donna Piscitelli (Our Sunday Visitor, 2009). This practical guide to the Beatitudes will delight the family as they learn the heart of Jesus' teaching about the Kingdom.

5. *Jesus Wants All of Me: Forgiveness,* Phil A. Smouse (Barbour Publishing, 2000). This is one title in a series of four books that children in primary school can read easily.

6. *What Did Jesus Do? Stories about Honesty and Forgiveness,* Mary Manz Simon (Thomas Nelson, 1998). These stories from the New Testament are presented attractively and engagingly for young children.

7. *Forgiving a Friend,* Virginia Kroll (Albert Whitman, 2005). This book presents parallel stories about ways children and adults deal with incidents that call for either anger or forgiveness.

8. *Child's Guide to Reconciliation,* Elizabeth Ficocelli (Paulist Press, 2003). Helping children develop confidence about the idea of reconciliation and the liturgy of the Sacrament, this text aims to create a joyful experience for the youngsters.

9. *Down the Road,* Alice Schertle (Sandpiper, 2000). A moral tale told in the context of family love considers the consequences of good and bad choices.

10. *Harriet, You'll Drive Me Wild!* Mem Fox (Harcourt, 2000). Learning to apologize to those we've disappointed does not mean that we risk being unloved.

11. *You'll Be Sorry,* Josh Schneider (Clarion Books, 2007). Sibling quarrels, even when described with humor, beg for apologies and reconciliation.

12. *I Call My Hand Gentle,* Amanda Haan (Viking, 2003). Treating others with respect is the beginning of learning how to make good choices. This story might be appropriate for beginning the examination of conscience during reconciliation services.

13. *If Peace Is . . . ,* Jane Baskwill (Mondo Publishing, 2003). Peace is not just a feeling of serenity; it is a virtue that needs to be practiced in everyday life.

14. *Stolen Smile,* Thierry Robberecht (Doubleday Books for Young Readers, 2000). This story shows the effect harmful words and actions can have on others. When we hurt each other, forgiveness is necessary.

A final note: In order to avoid the constant repetition of "your child" and to give recognition to both girls and boys, we will vary the personal pronouns in alternating chapters. In one chapter, we will use feminine pronouns (such as *she* and *hers*), and in the next chapter, we will use masculine pronouns (such as *he* and *his*).

Chapter

In the Name of the Father, and of the Son, and of the Holy Spirit

Parent Background: Freedom and Forgiveness

Many generations have passed since Adam and Eve made the choice that so affected their lives and ours. But our gifts and temptations are similar to theirs. We too have the gift of free will and we too can be tempted to misuse this gift. Even taking into consideration that our inner freedom may be compromised in some ways by our background or other innate tendencies, our gift of free will, if used wisely, can help us to stay close to God. Or, like Adam and Eve, we can use our freedom in selfish ways and hurt our relationship with God.

This great gift of free will is still ours today. In preparing young children for the Sacrament of Reconciliation, it is important to help them understand that they have choices. Because of Baptism, they have been given grace to choose rightly.

GET READY!

Recall the time of preparation for your child's Baptism, and the ways in which you envisioned bringing her up in the Catholic Church community. Reflect on things she identifies as part of being a Catholic.

GET SET!

If possible, place your child's baptismal candle in the prayer space along with a photo of the event. Place some examples of crosses there. Be sure to have art supplies and construction paper on hand.

Pray: Light the candle. Then say, "Let us begin our prayer in the name of the Father . . . ," and pray the Sign of the Cross together.

.... Page 1 ....

GO!

Focus attention on the photo and ask your child to describe what she sees.

Also explain that the Sign of the Cross is a very important prayer to Catholics because it reminds us of our Baptism and that we are followers of Jesus Christ.

Demonstrate how to make the Sign of the Cross with large gestures.

······· Pages 2 and 3 ·······

We Listen

Draw attention to the illustration on pages 2 and 3. Point out that this picture shows the first people God created. Then read together the Scripture about Adam and Eve in the Garden of Eden. Ask your child to retell the story in her own words.

Point out that Adam and Eve were happy living in the Garden of Eden.

Ask, "What did they do that caused them to be unhappy?" *(They decided to do what God had asked them not to do.)* Emphasize that they became unhappy because they had turned away from God's love.

Explain that Adam and Eve forgot how much God loved and cared for them. They hurt their friendship with God by disobeying his rules.

Activity

Read the activity directions. Give examples of actions that would lead us away from God, such as taking something that doesn't belong to us or calling someone names. Then ask her to describe ways of making peace. *(being sorry, doing something good for that person, a hug, a handshake, a high-five, etc.)* Invite your child to draw a picture to complete the activity.

With My Family

Going to the United States Conference of Catholic Bishops (USCCB) site to find a section of the New American Bible may seem complicated at first, but you will see that it is a convenient way to access the Scriptures. It is also important that your child recognize the Bible as the written Word, passed on throughout history.

Additional Activity

▸ Introduce a psalm that tells of God's goodness. Have the psalm verses below prepared on a sheet of paper. Ask your child to repeat them line by line after you.

Bless the Lord, my soul;

do not forget all the gifts of God,

who forgives all your sins

and fills your days with good things.

(Based on Psalm 103:2–3,5)

Help your child to paste the page on construction paper and place it in the prayer space.

······· Pages 4 and 5 ·······

We Learn

Read the title and the first paragraph on page 4. Explain the meaning of sin as presented in that paragraph. Sin harms our friendship with God and the special bond we share with one another as children of God.

Read the second paragraph. Encourage your child to recall what the first sin was.

Read the first paragraph on page 5. Remind your child that God sent his Son Jesus to show us how to avoid sin and follow God's will. Explain that, when God forgives us, we are reunited with God and others.

Read the remaining text. Explain that God's grace helps us to love and forgive others as Jesus taught us.

Explain that the Sacraments are *effective* signs. They do what they say they will do. They give us grace, or a share in God's life. The grace we

14 Celebrate and Remember: Reconciliation Home Guide

receive in the Sacraments comes from Jesus himself by the power of the Holy Spirit.

Activity

Share ideas about times when families might be peaceful and happy together. *(at a family reunion, a birthday party, a family vacation, or even helping out together at home)* Then ask your child to draw a picture of your family doing something happily together.

We Learn

Read together the title and the first paragraph on page 6.

Draw attention to the photos of the Sacraments of Christian Initiation on pages 4 and 5. (On page 4, clockwise from top: Confirmation, Baptism, Reconciliation. On page 5: the Eucharist.) Briefly explain each Sacrament.

Point out that the Sacrament of Baptism is the first Sacrament we receive. In Baptism all our sins are forgiven, including Original Sin.

Read the remaining text on page 6.

Emphasize that Baptism joins us to Christ and to one another. Explain that we take part in the Sacrament of Penance and Reconciliation in order to receive God's forgiveness for sins we commit after Baptism.

Share the meaning of the stained-glass art with your child. The hand of the priest is raised in a blessing of peace. The two keys are signs that the priest has the power and authority from God to forgive sins.

Read the paragraph under "Celebrating the Sacrament" on page 7. Invite your child to pray the Sign of the Cross with you.

Activity

Read the activity directions. Then invite your child to name as many things as she can think of about the Sacrament of Reconciliation. List each idea on a sheet of paper. Consider together words she might choose. *(happy, peaceful, joyful, loving)*

Living Our Faith

Read the paragraph. Guide your child in understanding how important it is to respond to God's gift of grace in the Sacraments. Stress that Jesus asks us to come to the Sacraments with an attitude of faith, believing in him and being ready to accept his gift of grace.

With My Family

As you look at photos and other remembrances of family Baptisms, point out the priest or deacon and the people who were present. Talk about ways each person has contributed to the family's happiness over the years.

Additional Activity

▸ Show your child different examples or pictures of crosses and crucifixes. Ask her to point out which ones she finds most appealing. Then ask her to draw one that she would like to keep as a reminder of the Sign of the Cross. Place her drawing in the prayer space near the other examples.

····· Pages 8 and 9 ·····

 ## We Live

Explain to your child that a heart-to-heart talk is a serious and truthful conversation. Explain that this page presents a heart-to-heart talk about hurt feelings and the need for reconciliation.

Talk about the ideas in the Heart to Heart section on page 8. Stress the importance of talking with a parent or trusted adult when feelings are hurt.

Talk about the two photos on this page. Ask your child to make up a "before" and "after" story about the photos.

Activity

Read together the directions for the activity on page 9. Talk about negative situations between people that need reconciliation. Then invite your child to complete the activity.

Saint Spotlight

Read aloud the paragraph about Saint Teresa of Ávila. Talk about some ways Saint Teresa lived a holy life. She prayed and she studied about God and prayer. She also wrote about changing our ways from selfishness to love of God and others.

With My Family

Again, look at the pictures of the Sacraments on pages 4 and 5. Share a positive personal experience about each one with your child. Assure her that you are truly happy to be helping her prepare for the Sacrament of Reconciliation.

Additional Activity

▸ Looking at photos of family Baptisms, review the Sacrament of Baptism. Help your child draw each part of the Sacrament as you discuss it:

- *Water* is the primary sign of the Sacrament.
- Anointing with *holy oils,* usually found in cruets or small bottles, is another important part of the Sacrament. The oil of catechumens is used as the person is welcomed. Later, another oil, the Sacred Chrism, seals the newly baptized person with the Holy Spirit.
- The *baptismal candle* is a sign of the light of Christ and of faith in him.
- The *white garment* is a sign of new life in Jesus Christ, now that all sin has been forgiven.

Reviewing the Lesson

Help your child to recall the key points learned in this lesson:

- The Sacraments give us grace, God's life in us.
- Sin hurts our relationship with God and the Church.
- The Sacrament of Reconciliation brings us back to God and the Church.

····· Page 10 ·····

 ## We Pray

Invite your child to describe the photograph on this page. *(The boy and girl might be holding their arms up to praise God for creating them.)*

Light your prayer candle. Take the part of "Leader," and explain that your child should read the parts for "All." Then pray the prayer together. (You both might want to stand and raise your arms, as in the photo, and pray the last paragraph, the "Glory be . . . ," together.)

16 *Celebrate and Remember: Reconciliation* Home Guide

Chapter 2

Trust in God's Mercy

Parent Background: Our Wonderful Father

Asking for his inheritance before his father had even died seems a particularly selfish and disrespectful thing for the Prodigal Son to do. The fact that the father went along with this plan only illustrates his generous love.

In this story, we are meant to identify with the younger son. We are meant to become aware that we have been given tremendous gifts, yet we often waste them. We give in to our desire for instant gratification. An opportunity to sin presents itself, and we sometimes take it. We are not quite the grown-ups we pretend to be.

But we have a wonderful Father! We have a Father who is rich in mercy and forgiveness, who runs to meet us on the road, welcomes us back, dresses us in fine clothes (like a baptismal garment, for example), and throws a celebration just for us!

GET READY!

Keep in mind your relationship in prayer with God our Father. Your child will better understand his relationship with God if you use concrete terms to describe the mutual love you share with your heavenly Father.

GET SET!

Have art supplies on hand.

.... Page 11 ....

GO!

Tell your child that today's prayer is based on a Psalm. Explain that the Psalms are found in the Old Testament and that many were written by a king named David. In this psalm, David expresses sorrow for a serious sin he committed and asks for God's mercy.

Ask your child to think of a selfish act or unkind words that hurt someone and for which he is sorry. Tell him that in this prayer he can ask God to forgive him.

Decide who will be the leader. Light the candle, begin with the Sign of the Cross, then alternate reading side 1 and side 2. Then pray the "All" section together.

Pages 12 and 13

We Listen

Explain that Jesus often told special stories called *parables* to help us grow closer to God. Sometimes the characters in the parables stand for someone else. In this Scripture story, the forgiving Father is God.

Read together "The Forgiving Father." Ask your child to retell the story in his own words. Point out that the father loved his children and took care of them. The younger son did not appreciate all that his father had given him. He thought only of himself. But when he realized he had sinned, he went home to tell his father he was sorry.

Direct attention to the illustration on pages 12 and 13. Point out that the father loves his son so much that he doesn't even wait for him to walk to the house. He rushes out to meet him. Invite your child to talk about other signs of the father's affection for his son.

Stress that we are God's children. God our Father rejoices when we are sorry for our sins and turn back to him. Recall the concept of reconciliation presented in chapter 1 and its fundamental meaning of being reunited with God and others.

Activity

Read together the words in the box on page 13. Explain the directions and do the first word of the puzzle together. Talk about your child's responses. Answers in order are: *Father, son, sorry, God, sin, love, rejoice.*

With My Family

As you read these stories together, ask your child to think of real-life experiences of the sorrow of loss and the joy of recovery. He will then be ready to understand that reconciliation involves two parts, and that sorrow and forgiveness are both needed.

Additional Activity

▶ Invite your child to retell the Parable of the Forgiving Father in his own words. Ask him to draw a map showing the father's house, the far-off country where the prodigal son went, and the distance in between. Then have him draw the father waiting outside his home for the son to return. Lastly, ask him to draw the son on the path back home.

Pages 14 and 15

We Learn

Read aloud the title and the first paragraph on page 14.

Point out that God sent his Son, Jesus Christ, to bring us back to God and save us from sin. Recall that the name Jesus means "God saves." Remind your child that Original Sin weakens our ability to avoid sin. Jesus Christ frees us from sin and reunites us with God and one another.

Read the next two paragraphs.

Emphasize that God the Father loves us; God welcomes us back when we are sorry for our sins.

Then read the paragraph on page 15.

Point out that the word *contrition* means being sorry for our sins and trying not to sin again.

Talk about some different reasons we can be sorry or have contrition for what we have said or done. Recall that we can be sorry because we love God and we love the person we have hurt. We can be sorry because we will be scolded or punished for what we did.

Point out that both ways of being sorry are contrition, but being sorry because we love God and the person we hurt is a better reason.

Emphasize that, in addition to being sorry for our sins, we must try not to sin again. Recall that Jesus gave us the Sacraments to help our relationship with God grow stronger. Prayer, talking with God often, also helps us stay close to God.

Activity

Read the activity directions. Then share together times to be sorry for what we do. *(fighting; teasing even when someone says, "Stop"; calling names; refusing to share games; not doing as parents ask or direct; not listening to teachers or other adults in charge)*

Ask your child to think about what he looks like when he is sorry. Ask him to draw himself looking sad.

Pages 16 and 17

We Learn

Read together the title and the first paragraph on page 16.

Point out that we first receive our new life in Christ when we are baptized.

Remind your child that Original Sin and all sins are forgiven at Baptism.

Read together the second paragraph on page 16.

Explain that our sins are forgiven in the Sacrament of Reconciliation through the words and actions of the priest or bishop.

Then emphasize that Jesus gave us the Sacrament of Penance and Reconciliation for the forgiveness of sins committed after Baptism. Recall that only God can forgive sins. Jesus Christ gave priests and bishops the power to forgive sins in his name.

Read the first paragraph under "Celebrating the Sacrament" on page 17. Explain that *mercy* means "God's love and forgiveness." Take turns pretending to be the priest and giving the response. In the Sacrament of Reconciliation, we trust God to love and forgive us.

Activity

Explain the directions for the art activity on page 17. Allow your child to color the letters of the hidden message.

Faith Highlights

Read together the Faith Highlights text. Share with your child that only priests and bishops have the power to forgive sins in Jesus' name in the Sacrament of Penance and Reconciliation.

With My Family

You might like to ask your child to underline two important sentences on these two pages. Suggested sentences are: page 16, paragraph 2, sentence 2 ("In this Sacrament . . .") and page 17, sentence 1 ("When we celebrate . . .").

Additional Activity

▸ Plan a visit to your church to give your child an up-close look at the worship area and the objects he may be familiar with from a distance. Point out the baptismal font or pool, the altar table, the tabernacle, and the Paschal candle.

You may also wish to introduce your child to the place where he will celebrate the Sacrament with the priest. Refer to the "Where We Celebrate Reconciliation" section on page 81 in the child's book.

Pages 18 and 19

We Live

Explain that this Heart to Heart page describes a beautiful gift. Read this section together.

Then discuss the photo by asking your child to describe what he sees. Ask him to guess what might be inside the beautiful box. Point out that at Baptism we received the gift of God's grace that helps us to make good choices.

Activity

Read together the directions for the maze activity. Offer to help your child complete the activity, if he needs assistance.

Saint Spotlight

Read together the paragraph about Saint Thérèse. Talk about the saint's life. Emphasize that Saint Thérèse did little things with great love, even when she was a little girl, and was quick to ask forgiveness when she did something wrong.

With My Family

Look up the lives of holy people such as Saint Jean Vianney, the Curé of Ars; Saint Stephen; Archbishop Oscar Romero of El Salvador; and Pope John Paul II.

Additional Activity

▸ Invite your child to put together a children's Bible storybook. Explain that the book should be directed to younger children who need to know about forgiveness.

Fold in half two sheets of paper to make an eight-page booklet. Invite your child to review the parts of the prodigal son story and draw them on successive pages. Have him title the pictures at the bottom.

Make a cover with construction paper, with the title, "A Story of Forgiveness."

Reviewing the Lesson

Help your child to recall the key points learned in this lesson:

- God forgives our sins when we are sorry, or have contrition.
- Contrition means being sorry and trying not to sin again.
- Our sins are forgiven in the Sacrament of Reconciliation.

Page 20

We Pray

Look together at the picture of the ocean. Explain that God's love is bigger than the ocean! The closing prayer is about having a forgiving heart. Light the candle, begin with the Sign of the Cross, and pray together.

20 *Celebrate and Remember: Reconciliation* Home Guide

Chapter 3

We Follow God's Word

Parent Background: A Light for My Path

Your word is a lamp for my feet / a light for my path. (Psalm 119:105)

We look to the Scriptures for inspiration, for hope, and even sometimes for a lifeline in our everyday lives. In the midst of tragedy, pain, suffering, and just plain frustration, we hear the Word of God, especially in Jesus, the Word, assuring us, "Behold, I am with you always, until the end of the age" (Matthew 28:20).

In the Scriptures we also find our moral compass, the light for our path that helps to form our conscience. In faith and prayer, we ponder the wisdom given to us in the Ten Commandments and in the teachings of Jesus. How can we act on this wisdom? How can we make it more a part of our lives?

As you prepare your child to hear this Word, particularly in the Sacrament of Penance and Reconciliation, and to put it into practice in her life, you may recall that you participate in the New Covenant to which the prophet Jeremiah looked forward: "I will place my law within them, and write it upon their hearts; I will be their God, and they shall be my people" (Jeremiah 31:33) says the Lord!

GET READY!

Recall several Scripture stories or verses that have inspired you over the years. Meditate on one or two that have been especially helpful.

GET SET!

Gather together art supplies, construction paper, scissors, and paste.

You may also want to have a child's Bible on hand.

GO!

Focus attention on the photo on page 21 and ask your child to describe what she sees. Point out or elicit that this person is reading and praying with the Word of God. Explain that the Word of God is written down in a book we call "the Bible." Then light the candle and ask your child to read all the "Reader" parts. Begin with the Sign of the Cross, take the part of the leader, and pray the prayer together.

Pages 22 and 23

We Listen

Introduce the Scripture by talking about the many ways laws or rules help us to get along with one another. Have your child suggest places where rules might be posted, such as classrooms, museums, parks, or other public areas.

Explain that we find God's rules in the Bible. Read the Scripture story on pages 22 and 23. Be sure to read the Ten Commandments slowly, for emphasis.

Explain that the first three commandments teach us to love and honor God. The other commandments show us how to love and respect our neighbor.

Draw attention to the illustration on page 23. Note that the Ten Commandments are written on the stone tablets.

Explain that Jesus helps us to understand the Ten Commandments. He makes known the full and complete meaning of God's rules. Then draw attention to the writing on the scroll. It is Jesus' New Commandment of Love.

Invite your child to find Jesus' New Commandment on page 22.

Activity

Invite your child to read Jesus' words from Mark 12:28–31 and John 13:34, which are found following the Ten Commandments on page 22.

Direct her to circle the most important word that Jesus taught us. *(love)* Invite her to draw a symbol for this word. Talk about symbols of the word *love:* a heart, a hug, a bouquet of flowers (usually roses).

With My Family

When making the suggested list, be sure to discuss practical examples for each item. The closer to home the idea is, the more likely it is that your child will take it to heart.

Additional Activity

▸ Prepare a piece of plain white paper to look like the Ten Commandments: fold it in half and draw an arc at the top of each side to make a rounded top, as for two tablets. Draw a line down the center. Across the top of the tablets, print "The Ten Commandments." Then list the Commandments on the "tablets." (You may want to look at page 85 in the back of the child's book for simplified wording.) Paste the page onto a sheet of construction paper and place it in the prayer space.

Pages 24 and 25

We Learn

Read together the title of this section on page 24. Recall that the Ten Commandments were given to Moses on stone tablets. Explain that God's rules are also written in the Bible. Hold up the Bible and show your child the page where the Ten Commandments are listed. *(See Exodus 20:1–17.)* Continue reading together the first two paragraphs.

Then read together the last paragraph of "The Scriptures Guide Us." Point out the section of the Bible that contains the four Gospels. Emphasize that Jesus followed God's rules perfectly and helps us to understand how we should love God and other people.

Read the title and the first paragraph on page 25. Emphasize the Great Commandment presented there. Jesus taught us the Great Commandment to help us follow God's rules. We find this commandment in the Gospels.

Then read together the second paragraph on this page. Point out that sin is a deliberate choice to say, do, or want something wrong. Provide examples of a mistake or an accident, such as accidentally breaking a dish.

Activity

Emphasize that a sin is a choice to do what a person knows is wrong. Talk about ideas for mistakes or accidents. Together, come up with some examples. Invite your child to draw herself making a mistake or accidentally causing a problem.

.... Pages 26 and 27 ....

We Learn

Read aloud the title of this section. Explain that when we refuse to follow God's will, we sin. Then read about the two kinds of sin. Explain the differences between mortal and venial sin.

Point out that a venial sin is less serious than a mortal sin. It weakens our relationship with God, but it does not separate us from God.

Read together "Celebrating the Sacrament" on page 27. Draw attention to the photos on pages 26 and 27. Ask, "What is the boy on page 26 thinking about?" *(He may be thinking that he is sorry for something he did.)* Then ask, "What is happening in the photo on page 27?" *(The priest is reading the Word of God during the Sacrament of Reconciliation.)* Ask, "Why is it important to read the Word of God?" *(We hear God's Word of love and forgiveness. The Word of God helps us to love God and one another.)*

Activity

Read the directions for the activity on page 27.

Then help your child find the New Commandment following the Ten Commandments on page 22. Circle the words your child should copy onto the Bible page to finish the commandment.

Living Our Faith

Read the paragraph. Talk about ways God helps us each day to be loving and forgiving people.

With My Family

If you have a child's Bible at home, you might suggest reading one story each evening at bedtime. Another way to incorporate Scripture into daily life would be to read a verse at the family meal from the responsorial psalm for the upcoming Sunday Eucharist.

Additional Activity

› Invite your child to imagine that she and her friends are starting their own club. Explain that all groups have rules.

Ask her to name some of her friends that would be in the club. Then ask her to write out a list of rules for the club. Discuss the reason for each rule.

Then talk about rules that are not written down, but that everyone is expected to keep. Ask where these rules might come from. Note that some may be part of the Ten Commandments, and some may be from Jesus' New Commandment to love God and others.

··········⌣ Pages 28 and 29 ⌢··········

We Live

Share the ideas in the Heart to Heart text. Call attention to the photo. Help your child remember occasions when your family had a good and happy time together. Recall acts of kindness that show how much love there is among family members. Explain that we can follow the Ten Commandments AND Jesus' commandment to love God and to love others. The Ten Commandments are particular ways in which we can show our love for one another.

Activity

Read the introduction to this activity. Elicit reasons why each rule is a good one. Talk about good rules that we follow in our everyday lives and why they are good rules. Help your child think of a good and helpful rule to write down and explain at the bottom of the activity box.

Saint Spotlight

Read the paragraph about the featured saint. Talk about the honesty of Saint Dismas. He knew he had done wrong. He asked Jesus to forgive him and to bring him to Heaven. Saint Dismas teaches us that we can always be truthful. We can always ask Jesus for forgiveness.

With My Family

Family meetings can be an important segment of family life, especially during times of transition (before school begins for the year, when a long vacation starts, before holidays, and so on). Family meetings can be planning sessions for family events or can introduce changes in routine so that everyone's needs can be heard and taken into account. Some families have short weekly meetings to mark the family calendar.

Additional Activity

▶ Make a list of actions that would be considered as going against the Ten Commandments. Include especially acts or omissions that would be typical of children. Ask your child to identify which of the Commandments would apply in each case. Then ask what the right choice would have been in each instance.

Reviewing the Lesson

Help your child to recall the key points learned in this lesson:

- God revealed his rules to Moses in the Ten Commandments.
- The Great Commandment that Jesus taught is to love God and to love others.
- We find these Commandments and teachings in the Bible, which is also called the Scriptures. The Bible is the Word of God.

··········⌣ Page 30 ⌢··········

We Pray

Call attention to the photo of the child reading the Bible. Explain that the closing prayer is about asking God to help us follow his Word. Light the candle. Begin with the Sign of the Cross, and then pray the prayer together.

Chapter 4

I Confess

Parent Background: Staying Afloat

The images of ships and water and even shipwreck seem appropriate for the Sacrament of Penance and Reconciliation. We approach the Sacrament of Reconciliation to keep our ships turned in the right direction, to stay afloat on the seas of life. The Sacrament of Reconciliation assures us that we are not sailing alone on these choppy seas. This Sacrament gives us the opportunity to head for quiet harbor, to drop anchor for awhile, to assess our journey, and to be forgiven for any deliberate forays into dangerous waters.

Our children and others their age have never come near to wrecking their boats. But the grace of the Sacrament of Reconciliation is offered to them as well. They too are sailing choppy seas, in their own ways. The Sacrament of Reconciliation is offered to them because God cares about their journeys too. The Church is here for our children, to communicate God's message of love and forgiveness in this most personal way.

GET READY!

Consider times that were marked by confusion and doubt in your life. Be thankful for the graces that God has given to guide you in the right direction.

GET SET!

Have ready a piece of 8½-by-11-inch paper cut in the shape of a heart.

Page 31

GO!

Focus attention on the photo and ask your child to describe what he sees. Point out that the photo shows a mother hugging a child. Explain that the love of parents for children is a sign of God's love for us. In today's prayer we will learn what to do when we need God's love and forgiveness. Light the candle. Explain to your child that you and he will take turns being "Reader." Then take the part of "Leader," and pray the prayer together.

Give your child the paper heart you prepared and a pencil. Ask him to write a note to God telling God one way he would like to change to become more loving and caring. Tell your child that his note is private and should be put in a special place where he can read it each day.

Chapter 4 • I Confess 25

Pages 32 and 33

We Listen

Read aloud the Scripture story.

Explain that God wants us to take a careful look at the way we live. Preparing for the Lord includes looking into our hearts and admitting our sins. We think about ways we can better show our love for God and one another.

Invite your child to look at the illustration on pages 32 and 33 showing Jesus after he was baptized.

Explain that the dove above Jesus is a sign that Jesus was anointed by the Holy Spirit and that the Holy Spirit was with Jesus in a special way. Share that when we were baptized, the Holy Spirit was present, and that we were anointed with a sacred oil called "chrism." The Holy Spirit stays with us to help us to stay close to God and to love and forgive one another.

Explain that the voice of the Father made clear that he was pleased with Jesus, his only Son. God the Father wants us to listen to his Son, Jesus.

Activity

Ask your child to show how he can prepare his life for the Lord by drawing a picture illustrating his ideas. Help him to think of ways he helps others in his family, among his friends, or in the neighborhood. Help him choose one of these ways for his picture, and remind him that when he does good things for others, he is sharing God's goodness and love.

With My Family

As you share your child's drawing with the family, ask each family member to make a practical resolution for helping others that can be carried out this week. Ask family members to write out their resolutions, place them by their bedside, and refer to them each morning.

Additional Activity

> Remind your child of the prayers we pray at the beginning of Mass. We pray "Lord, have mercy" and "Christ, have mercy" *(Roman Missal)* as we ask forgiveness for whatever we may have done wrong. Make up personal petitions *("I am sorry, Lord, for being impatient in traffic today")* and encourage your child to do the same. Pray "Lord, have mercy" and "Christ, have mercy" in response.

Pages 34 and 35

We Learn

Read together the title and the first paragraph of this section. Draw attention to the word *repentance* in the last sentence of the paragraph. Stress that *repentance* and *contrition* mean the same thing. Explain that John the Baptist helps us to understand what *repent* means. John the Baptist wanted people to realize that sinning hurts our relationship with God. He asked people to make changes. But before we can change, we must first admit that we have done wrong.

Then continue reading the next paragraph. Focus attention on the word *confession*. Explain that it is important for us to confess our sins to a priest, because saying our sins out loud shows that we understand that we have sinned. After reading the paragraph, ask your child to explain in his own words what *confession* means.

Read aloud the first paragraph on page 35 together. Recall that when the priest listens to our confession, he is acting in the name of Jesus Christ. The priest helps us to start over again by giving us a penance to complete. He also may remind us that we need to be reconciled to those whom we may have hurt.

Be sure your child understands what a penance is and what it might include.

Read the last paragraph. Explain that in the Sacrament of Reconciliation, we repent, confess our sins, and do our penance. The Sacrament is completed when the priest absolves us, or forgives our sins.

Activity

Read the directions for the activity. With your child, make a list of some gifts of God, especially gifts to your family. Invite your child to include these gifts in their pictures of God's love for them.

Pages 36 and 37

We Learn

Read the first paragraph of "Our Conscience Guides Us." Explain that our conscience is a gift from God. It is a special kind of "knowing."

Read the remaining paragraphs. Stress paragraph 2, which lists the ways we can help our conscience to grow.

Read the two paragraphs under "Celebrating the Sacrament" on page 37. Point out that making an examination of conscience is the best way to prepare for the Sacrament of Reconciliation.

Explain that in an examination of conscience, we think about what we have done or not done to follow God's rules in the Ten Commandments and in the teachings of Jesus. Have your child recall from chapter 3 the Great Commandment and the New Commandment that Jesus taught us.

Activity

Help your child find the secret message to God in the puzzle on page 37. Ask him to color the spaces marked with an x.

Faith Highlights

Read together the paragraph. Share with your child that the priest must keep secret all sins he hears in the Sacrament of Penance and Reconciliation.

With My Family

Keep in mind that not all conversions are dramatic. Children's moral sense and motivation are closely tied to learning opportunities. It's more effective to ask, "What did you learn when . . . ?" as an example of change. You can help your child to understand by sharing some of your own conversions: finding a better way to deal with anger, quitting smoking or drinking, making time for exercise, incorporating other good habits into your life.

Additional Activity

▸ Help your child to make an examination of conscience. Direct him to page 84 in the back of his book. Ask him to listen carefully to each question. Read the examination of conscience slowly, pausing after each question to allow time for him to think about these questions and ways he could have been a better disciple of Jesus.

······ Pages 38 and 39 ······

 ## We Live

Explain to your child that this Heart to Heart talk is about a big secret. Ask him to listen carefully as you read so that he will know what the secret is. Talk about how people feel about things they have done that they know are wrong or hurtful. Explain that we have to admit our bad choices in order to be sorry for them. Examining our conscience helps us to think clearly about our actions.

Activity

Draw attention to the matching activity on page 39. Read together the directions. Then read together the words in the box. Slowly read each definition, and give your child time to find the word and write its number in the heart.

Saint Spotlight

Read the paragraph about Saint Anthony. Talk about Saint Anthony's way of life: He lived alone in the desert and prayed. Point out that Saint Anthony is an example of what should be most important in our lives: talking to and listening to God in our hearts, and always turning back to God.

With My Family

Talk with your family about ways of resolving conflict that work well, and those that have failed. Remember that most conflicts should be resolved at the level they occur, without appeal to higher authority. It's also helpful to focus on the present problem and avoid bringing up the past.

Additional Activity

▸ Invite your child to help you make a list of conflicts between family members or friends that frequently occur. For each item on the list, talk about strategies for avoiding the conflict. Then discuss ways of resolving the conflict so that it is unlikely to recur. Pray for the Holy Spirit to help in times of conflict.

Reviewing the Lesson

Help your child to recall the key points learned in this lesson:

- Repentance, like contrition, means that we are truly sorry for our sins and will try not to sin again.
- Telling our sins to the priest is called *confession.*
- An examination of conscience is thinking about our actions and any sins we may have committed.

······ Page 40 ······

 ## We Pray

Look together at the photo and ask what the children might be saying.

Explain that the closing prayer is a prayer to God our Father. Point out to your child that this is the prayer Jesus taught us, called the Lord's Prayer, or the Our Father. Light the candle, take the part of the leader, and pray together. End with the Sign of the Cross.

28 *Celebrate and Remember: Reconciliation* Home Guide

Chapter 5

I Am Sorry

Parent Background: Doing Penance

The Sacrament of Penance and Reconciliation seems to be the most intangible Sacrament of all. There is no water, no oil. There is no sharing of a sacred meal. There is no vow spoken, except the promise not to sin again. Yet God is here. And for the absolution, God's forgiveness is spoken in quiet blessing, with the outstretched hand of the priest hovering over the bowed head of the penitent.

Of course, absolution is not enough. Absolution does take away sin, but not all the "disorders" that the sin has brought about. We must do our part. Penance is that part. Even a child understands the fairness of this. The Sacrament of Reconciliation heals us, but then, through our willingness to change, we take responsibility for healing the disorders our sin has caused.

GET READY!

When we are sorry for having done wrong, we often seek some gesture of our repentance. In some cases, we try to make up for having done harm. We may decide to correct damage done or perform an act of kindness. Recall these times as you explain the notion of penance in this lesson.

GET SET!

Gather art supplies including the following: purple construction paper, an Act of Contrition printed out in large letters on 8½-by-11-inch printer paper, black crayons, and paste or glue.

Add to the prayer table a statue of Mary and a small empty vase.

.... Page 41 ....

GO!

Light the prayer candle. Explain to your child that in this prayer you will be reading the side 1 parts of the Act of Contrition and that she will be reading the side 2 parts. Then repeat the prayer, taking the opposite parts.

Focus attention on the photo in her book. Point out that the boy is celebrating the Sacrament of Penance and Reconciliation and is speaking with the priest. Explain that when we sin, God still loves us. He wants to forgive us. He wants us to be sorry. One way we can tell God we are sorry is by praying a prayer of sorrow called an Act of Contrition.

····· Pages 42 and 43 ·····

We Listen

Discuss the picture on pages 42 and 43 by asking: "What does the woman in the picture appear to be doing?" *(She is washing Jesus' feet with her tears.)*

"Why do you think the woman is crying?" *(Accept all reasonable responses.)*

Introduce the Scripture story on page 42 by asking your child to listen carefully to find out more about the woman—who she is and why she is weeping. Explain that in the country where Jesus lived, the weather was warm most of the time, and people wore sandals. Their feet got very dirty. In the time of Jesus, washing feet was a way to welcome guests.

Point out that the Pharisees looked down on the woman because of her sins. Jesus, however, was kind and compassionate to her. He saw that her kind acts showed how sorry she was for her sins.

Activity

Read the directions for the activity on page 43. Brainstorm possible words: *happy, hopeful, glad, peaceful, and so on.* Write these on a piece of paper.

Then instruct your child to choose some of these words and write them in the box.

With My Family

The parable Jesus told Simon is found in Luke 7:40–43. After reading the story, help your child picture this parable by writing "500 days' wages" and "50 days' wages" on a piece of paper. Then estimate what these might amount to, using an average daily wage today. Jesus explains the lesson to Simon in verse 47. This story reminds us that God looks not at our sin, however great or small it is, but at our love.

Additional Activity

▸ Direct your child to paste the Act of Contrition (already written out) on the piece of purple construction paper by putting a dab of paste in each corner.

Have her fold the construction paper, with the prayer inside, in half, like a card.

Suggest that she pray the Act of Contrition each night. If appropriate, she might bring the prayer to First Reconciliation with her.

····· Pages 44 and 45 ·····

We Learn

Read aloud the title and the first two paragraphs of "We Are Sorry for Our Sins" to help your child understand the connection between the Scripture story and the Sacrament of Penance and Reconciliation. Point out that Jesus has mercy on sinners who have faith in him and sorrow for their sins.

Explain that we are *penitents* because we seek forgiveness for our sins. Jesus gave us the Sacrament of Reconciliation so we could ask for and receive his mercy and forgiveness.

Then read together the last paragraph on page 44. Emphasize that part of showing sorrow for our sins is deciding not to sin again and doing things that help us to avoid sin.

Continue reading the paragraph on page 45. Remind your child that Jesus gave all priests

30   *Celebrate and Remember: Reconciliation* Home Guide

the power to forgive sins so that we can hear with our own ears that God loves us and forgives us.

Activity

Read aloud the directions for the activity on page 45.

Ask your child to tell when and where she talks to Jesus. Talk about ideas for times and places (for example, before going to bed, while waiting for the school bus, while riding in the car, etc.). Invite her to draw a picture of herself talking to Jesus. Remind her to ask Jesus to help her and to be with her when she comes as a penitent to the Sacrament of Reconciliation.

Pages 46 and 47

We Learn

Read aloud the title and the three paragraphs on page 46.

Recall that the priest helps us after we confess our sins by encouraging us to follow Jesus. He also gives us a penance. Review the three important actions we take as penitents in the Sacrament of Reconciliation: We show contrition or sorrow for our sins, we confess our sins to a priest, we do a penance.

Then read together the paragraph on page 47. Plan a time together to go over the words of the Act of Contrition with your child. Find out whether she is expected to memorize this prayer for First Reconciliation, or if reading it (from a prayer card or from the First Reconciliation child's book) is an option. The Act of Contrition can be found on page 41 in the child's book or on page 92 in the back of the book.

Activity

Read together and explain the directions for the activity on page 47.

Work together to find the letter for the first symbol, and have your child write the letter on the line. (*The answer to the secret code is* "Act of Contrition.")

Living Our Faith

Read the paragraph together. Emphasize the word *absolution* and invite your child to repeat it after you. Explain that *absolution* means "forgiveness."

With My Family

Be sure that this prayer is brief and non-specific regarding individuals. If it is brief enough, family members might use it as part of apologies for doing wrong to others.

Additional Activity

▸ Explain to your child that *virtue* means "strength" and is the habit of doing good. The more virtuous, or strong, a person is, the less likely she is to make poor or harmful choices. Both good and bad habits are hard to break, because they become automatic.

Identify good and bad habits. Explain that good habits in our moral behavior can be developed through practice. You may each want to choose a good habit or virtue (listening to others, doing as Mom or Dad asks at the first request, closing doors quietly, being on time, etc.) to practice this week. Make a pact to remind each other of this new good habit you are practicing!

Pages 48 and 49

 ## We Live

Before reading this Heart to Heart section, introduce the idea of fairness. After reading or discussing the ideas in the Heart to Heart section, explain that in the Sacrament of Reconciliation, we receive a penance from the priest. The penance helps us to make up for what is lacking in our behavior, even in a little way.

Activity

Read together the story about Ramón and his brother, including the questions at the end of the story. Discuss possible endings. What does Ramón's brother say and do? Direct your child to write an ending for the story.

Saint Spotlight

Read together the paragraph about the greatest saint, Mary. Talk about ways that Mary, the Mother of God and our mother too, lived a holy life. Being conceived and born without Original Sin was Mary's greatest privilege. This favor of God prepared her to be the mother of his Son. Yet, though being sinless herself, she has great compassion for sinners.

With My Family

Talk about ways that family members can put disputes and hurts behind them and start over with good feelings, respect, and a willingness to be helpful.

Additional Activity

▶ Explain that part of showing that we are sorry for our sins is to take responsibility for our actions. Responsibility means doing what is right without being told or reminded.

Review all the things that adults in the family take responsibility for: work, meals, cleaning, transportation, etc. Ask whether your child feels ready to contribute responsibly at home. Suggest ideas like keeping her room clean, setting the table, drying dishes, caring for a pet, etc. You might want to have her print her responsibilities on a calendar.

Reviewing the Lesson

Help your child to recall the key points learned in this lesson:

- Jesus gave his Church the power to forgive sins in his name.
- In the Sacrament of Reconciliation, we are sorry for our sins and pray an Act of Contrition.
- We do our penance to show we are sorry and to make up for our sins.

Page 50

 ## We Pray

Explain that placing flowers near a statue of Mary is a way of honoring her as the Mother of God.

Begin with the Sign of the Cross. Invite your child to place a flower in the vase near Mary's statue. Encourage her to ask Mary to help her always choose to do what is good. Light the candle. Then pray the Hail Mary together.

Chapter 6

Pardon and Peace

Parent Background: Go Find Jesus

Zacchaeus was small, and he had great humility. He did not care what people thought of him. He wanted to see Jesus, and he was not too proud to climb a tree to do it.

But Zacchaeus got more than he expected. He wanted to see Jesus; he did not expect to hear Jesus speak to him personally as well. And he did not expect to be visited in his own home by this eminent Teacher. But Jesus did speak. And Jesus did visit. And Jesus did grant Zacchaeus forgiveness and salvation.

And Jesus will speak to us. He will ask us to come down from our heights, to "get down to earth" in our examination of conscience, and to confess our sins with true sorrow. And then, at the prayer of absolution, God—the Father, the Son, and the Holy Spirit—will indeed visit us. God will bring us pardon and peace.

GET READY!

It is perhaps one of the most difficult challenges of parenthood to accept that our children will learn that we are not perfect. The fact that we can admit our failings will encourage our children to come to grips with their own failings and be truthful about their behavior.

GET SET!

Have crayons, scissors, and some drawing paper available. Add to the prayer table a live green plant and a glass pitcher of water.

GO!

Focus attention on the photo and ask your child to describe what he sees. Explain that the handshake is a sign of peace and good will that we often see around us, and at the Sign of Peace at Mass as well. Then light the candle. Sing or read the words of the song together prayerfully. Prompt your child to give examples of how he can let peace flow out of himself to bring peace to others. Remind him that when God forgives our sins in the Sacrament of Penance, he gives us the gift of peace. Hold up the pitcher of water. As you water the plant, remind your child that both we and the plant need water to grow and stay alive. Ask, "What do we need to grow as God wants?" *(peace, faith, hope, and love)*

Pages 52 and 53

We Listen

Direct attention to the illustration on pages 52 and 53. Ask your child to notice the crowds surrounding Jesus.

Then introduce your child to the character Zacchaeus, who climbed a tree to see Jesus.

Read together the Scripture account of Zacchaeus. Ask your child to retell the story in his own words. Emphasize that Zacchaeus trusted in God's mercy. He wanted to tell Jesus he was sorry for his sins.

Point out that Zacchaeus wanted to be close to Jesus. When Zacchaeus repented, Jesus forgave his sins so that he could begin a new life with God.

Activity

On page 53, direct your child to silently read and respond to the first question related to the story of Zacchaeus: What did Zacchaeus do? *(He gave half of what he had to the poor and paid back all the money he had stolen.)*

Direct your child to find the answer to the fill-in-the-blank quotation near the end of the Scripture story.

Briefly explain the word *salvation* (the answer to this activity).

Emphasize that when we have a loving relationship with God, we have salvation, just as Zacchaeus did.

With My Family

Ask for concrete examples of lost keys, lost homework, etc. Suggest that people too can become lost when they choose to do what is wrong and harmful. In the Sacrament of Reconciliation, Jesus calls back to him those who have lost their way.

Additional Activity

> Explain that almost everyone has limitations. Some, like Zacchaeus, have physical limitations, like blindness or paralysis. Others have learning challenges.
>
> Like Zacchaeus, however, we can all decide to do our best. But we may need some help from time to time. Talk about ways you, your child, and your family overcome difficulties. Then talk about ways you can help others overcome their limitations.

Pages 54 and 55

We Learn

Read the title and the first two paragraphs of "Jesus Brings Salvation" on page 54.

Recall with your child that our conscience guides us in knowing when we have sinned. Point out that our conscience helps us to take responsibility for our sins and to make things right again with God and the people we hurt. Stress that sin hurts our relationship with God and with one another. But Jesus looks for us when we have lost our way. He wants us to live in friendship with God and in peace with one another.

Explain that *salvation* is God's love and forgiveness of our sins.

Read the last paragraph on page 54. Point out that Jesus gave us the Sacrament of Penance and Reconciliation, in which we receive God's forgiveness in *absolution*.

Then read the paragraph on page 55. Explain that God's gift of peace comforts us and helps us to begin our new life with him. His grace is within us, guiding us to be more loving and forgiving.

Activity

Read the directions for the activity on page 55.

Remind your child that the Sign of the Cross is the sign that Jesus died and rose for us, so that we could share his life and his peace. Invite him to draw himself showing God that he is thankful for his peace. Talk about ways to show this. *(being kind to others, forgiving others, spending time talking and listening to God in prayer, singing a happy song for God, using our talents to make others happy, etc.)*

We Learn

Read aloud the title and the first paragraph of "Celebrating the Sacrament" on page 56. Then, as you read the next paragraph, ask your child to pretend that he has just confessed his sins and prayed an Act of Contrition. Now he will receive absolution from the priest. Then hold out your right hand over your child, as in the photo, and read the prayer. Remind your child to say "Amen" at the end.

Emphasize that Jesus Christ, through the words and actions of the priest, absolves us, or forgives us, of our sins.

Continue by reading the paragraph on page 57. Stress that after the Sacrament of Reconciliation, we are closer to Jesus, and are ready to follow him again.

Activity

Read the activity directions.

Invite your child to complete the message that tells us about the gifts we receive from God through the priest's prayer of absolution. (The answers to the puzzle are *pardon, peace,* and *reconciled.*)

Faith Highlights

Review the meaning of *grace.* (See the glossary, page 94.) Emphasize that every Sacrament changes us because every Sacrament gives us God's life. Recall that the Sacrament of Reconciliation gives us peace, and other gifts we will learn about in the next chapter.

With My Family

Point out that peace, to a degree, can be achieved silently and personally. Harmony, on the other hand, requires cooperation. The idea of reconciliation is to bring us together with others and with God, our forgiving Father.

Additional Activity

▸ Talk with your child about signs of reconciliation that he may observe or experience, like handshakes or hugs.

Point out that it is sometimes customary for people to exchange gifts, like cards or flowers, as symbols of reconciliation.

On a piece of drawing paper, have your child draw a wrapped gift. Then have him cut it out. On one side of the picture, have him print, "I'm sorry," and on the other, "I forgive you."

You may want to place this "gift" in a prominent place. Ask family members to exchange it, as a helpful prompt, when apologies are needed.

> Pages 58 and 59

We Live

Explain that this Heart to Heart talk is about peace—peace with God and peace with others. Read this section aloud.

Then draw attention to the photo on this page. Emphasize that it is always good to talk to a parent or trusted adult when we have any kind of difficulty.

Activity

Read aloud the directions for the activity on page 59.

Ask your child to recall large advertisements on billboards he has seen along the highway. Then direct his attention to the billboard drawn on this page. Ask him to write or draw in this billboard one way he can work for peace.

Saint Spotlight

Read together the paragraph about Saint Richard of Chichester. Talk about the holy life of Saint Richard. He studied to become a lawyer, but became a priest and bishop instead. His prayer on page 93 in the back of the child's book was the inspiration for the song "Day by Day."

With My Family

If you plan to attend the parish communal celebration of Reconciliation, review beforehand the steps of the ritual. At the celebration, explain to your child what is happening at each part of the liturgy.

Stress that although it is most common for people to participate in the Sacrament in private, the presence of the community is a strong reminder that what we do always affects the entire Body of Christ, the whole Church.

Additional Activity

> A dove is the sign of the Holy Spirit and a sign of peace. Draw an outline of a dove on a piece of paper. On it, ask your child to write something from this lesson that impressed him in some way (perhaps a verse from the opening prayer, what Jesus said to Zacchaeus, or the words of absolution). Cut out the dove and hang it from the ceiling in your child's room as a sign of the peace of the Sacrament of Reconciliation.

Reviewing the Lesson

Help your child to recall the key points learned in this lesson:

- Jesus wants us to have salvation.
- In the Sacrament of Reconciliation, we are given absolution, or forgiveness of our sins.
- The Sacrament of Reconciliation brings us pardon and peace.

> Page 60

We Pray

Ask your child to look at and describe the photo on page 60. Point out that giving food to the poor is something that Saint Richard did and that it is one of the Works of Mercy. Explain that Saint Richard wrote the closing prayer just before he died. Explain that the word *Redeemer* is another word for *Savior*. Jesus is our Redeemer. Light the candle, pray the Sign of the Cross, and then pray this prayer together.

36 *Celebrate and Remember: Reconciliation* Home Guide

Chapter 7

His Mercy Endures Forever

Parent Background: The Good Shepherd

Our understanding of shepherds in the Scriptures can be somewhat conditioned by the image of the humble, poor shepherds on Christmas cards and carols. The image that Jesus presents, however, is that of the brave and loyal shepherd who endures hardships and dangers to care for his flock. The story of King David cannot have been far from the minds of his hearers.

Jesus tells of a shepherd who is so dedicated to the care of each individual sheep that he will leave the rest on their own to rescue even one who is lost. He will bring the sheep back amid rejoicing. Of course, Jesus is really speaking about us as sinners that sometimes wander off, separate ourselves from the protection of the shepherd and the flock. He will always seek us out to bring us back.

Your child has already experienced this kind of unselfish and courageous love within your family. She also needs to be reassured that God's love and forgiveness are unconditional, and that that love and forgiveness is abundantly given in the Sacrament of Penance and Reconciliation.

GET READY!

Consider the many times we have felt Jesus calling us back when we were in need of reconciliation with others. We are always aware that a change of heart is possible with his help.

GET SET!

Have art supplies available.

Add to the prayer space a statue or picture of Jesus the Good Shepherd carrying a sheep on his shoulders.

GO!

Focus attention on the photo. Suggest to your child that the boy in the photo is praising God for his mercy and for all his creation.

Point out that in the opening prayer, we will thank God for his wonderful gifts, especially the gift of his mercy, or loving forgiveness. Light the candle. Ask your child to be the "Reader." Take the part of "Leader," and pray the prayer together.

····· Pages 62 and 63 ·····

 ## We Listen

Direct attention to the illustration. Ask, "Why do you think the shepherd is carrying a sheep on his shoulders?" Point out how happy the shepherd looks holding the sheep.

Explain that Jesus is our Good Shepherd. Invite your child to listen to the Scripture story about Jesus, the Good Shepherd.

After reading, explain that Jesus told the story of the Good Shepherd to help the Pharisees and scribes understand that God cares for all people. God especially wants to help those who have sinned and lost their way. Point out that the shepherd cared for and protected all his sheep. The one sheep that became lost needed his help. The shepherd called his friends and neighbors together because he wanted them to celebrate with him about having found the lost sheep. God never stops loving us, even when we sin. He rejoices when we repent and turn back to him.

Activity

Read the activity directions on page 63. Ask your child to color the letters that show Jesus' message to us. Invite her to read the message aloud. Remind her that our sins are forgiven in the Sacrament of Reconciliation.

With My Family

Once you have composed the prayer together, print it out and display it on the refrigerator or in another prominent place in your home. If you wish, you can use the prayer at mealtime as part of the grace or blessing.

Additional Activity

▸ Explain to your child that Jesus told the story of the Good Shepherd to people who were very familiar with herds of sheep and their shepherds. If Jesus were telling the story today, what other familiar "good" people might he use? Ask, "Who are some of the people who are responsible for looking after us?" *(Answers might include teachers, police officers, fire fighters, doctors, nurses, crossing guards, school bus drivers, etc.)* Invite your child to tell a story about one of these people caring for children.

····· Pages 64 and 65 ·····

 ## We Learn

Read the title and the first paragraph on page 64.

Point out that Jesus loves us, even when we sin. He is the Good Shepherd who never stops searching for us when we stray.

Then read the second paragraph. Explain that the Church is the community of believers. The Church was begun by Jesus Christ, and is united to him. When we sin, we hurt our relationship with God and with all the people who belong to the Church. The good things we do help all of us, and the sins we commit hurt all of us.

Recall that through the Sacrament of Penance and Reconciliation, we can receive God's forgiveness. Through this Sacrament we are brought back to God and the Church. Grace helps us to follow Jesus more closely. It gives us the strength to do what is right and to make good choices.

Continue by reading the first paragraph on page 65. Direct attention to the photos on pages 64 and 65. Discuss how each photo shows people at peace with God, with themselves, or with others. Point out that God's gift of peace brings us joy and happiness now and forever.

Help your child to recall from chapter 6 that the gift of a peaceful conscience means that sin no longer drags us down. We are free of our sins and rise to a new life with Jesus.

Then read the last paragraph on this page. Talk about how happy we are to have Jesus as our Good Shepherd!

Activity

Read aloud the activity directions on page 65. Allow your child to work independently on the maze. Offer help if needed.

·············: Pages 66 and 67 :·············

We Learn

Direct attention to the list of gifts of the Sacrament of Reconciliation on page 66. After you read together each gift, ask your child to say a bit more about it to be sure she has grasped the concept.

Read the sentence below the list. Stress that grace, which is God's life within us, keeps us close to him. His grace gives us the strength to seek his forgiveness when we sin.

Direct attention to "Celebrating the Sacrament" on page 67. Read the first paragraph. Then read the priest's part of the prayer of praise and thanks that follows absolution. Invite your child to pray the penitent's response.

Activity

Prepare your child for the activity by reminding her that peace is an inner calm that results from the forgiveness of sins. You may wish to have her look again at the photos on these two pages for examples of people at peace.

Encourage her to complete the sentence and to draw a picture showing a time when she feels at peace.

Living Our Faith

Read together the Living Our Faith text. Discuss the Church's teachings on how often we should receive the Sacrament of Reconciliation. You may want to discuss other precepts. The Precepts of the Church can be found on page 87.

With My Family

Discuss with your family ways in which the gifts of the Sacrament can be realized in everyday life.

Additional Activity

▸ Explain to your child that whenever we receive a Sacrament, our whole Church community also receives the grace of that Sacrament to help us live up to what we have received. Just as in Baptism, when our godparents and families shared in this grace with our whole parish, so in Reconciliation we have confidence that we will have the prayers and support we need to live as Jesus' disciples.

Think about and list the names of people in the community who are good examples to us and who may help us live a more holy life. Compose a prayer of thanksgiving for their help and support.

.... Pages 68 and 69 ....

 ## We Live

Read aloud the Heart to Heart section. Talk about the feelings of being lost and then being found. Recall that the shepherd's job is to keep the flock together, to lead them to good food and water, and to find the sheep that are lost. That is Jesus' job too. But he does not take care of sheep. He takes care of us! In Reconciliation, Jesus calls us back when we have lost our way.

Activity

Read together the directions for the activity. Explain that this place could be real or it could be imaginary. Allow your child to work independently. When she is finished, ask her to share and explain what she has drawn.

Saint Spotlight

Read together the paragraph about Saint Joseph. Talk about Saint Joseph's holy life. He followed God's way even when he didn't understand the full meaning of what God was asking him to do. He took care of Mary and Jesus as best he could. He taught Jesus how to be a carpenter.

With My Family

Discuss with your family times when they have judged others or their behavior for superficial reasons. How did those in your family feel when they found out that they were wrong? Getting to know others is the key to respect and understanding.

Additional Activity

▸ Invite your child to compose a story in three parts.

Part one should be about a child her age making a poor choice that does some harm to another person. Have her describe the child's reasons for making that poor choice.

Part two should be about how this same child might have realized that she had harmed her relationship with God and with the person whom she hurt. Did anyone help her understand about her wrong choice?

Part three should be about how the child decided to make things right and was reconciled to the other person and to God. What was the outcome of her decision?

Reviewing the Lesson

Help your child to recall the key points learned in this lesson:
- Jesus is the Good Shepherd.
- In the Sacrament of Reconciliation, we are given many gifts.
- In the Sacrament of Reconciliation, after absolution, we praise and thank God.

.... Page 70 ....

 ## We Pray

Explain that the closing prayer is about Jesus the Good Shepherd. Tell your child that it is an echo prayer, which means that you will take the part of the leader and that she should "echo," or repeat, the words she hears. Light the candle. Then begin by praying the Sign of the Cross together.

Chapter

Go in Peace

Parent Background: Rejoice and Exult!

Two of the most common phrases in the Bible are "Be not afraid" and "Peace be with you." This lesson emphasizes the joy and peace that are gifts of the Sacrament of Reconciliation. It links the Sacrament of Reconciliation to Baptism and the new life of Easter, and affirms that we are "Easter people" who rejoice that the Risen Christ is with us always.

Fear of making mistakes and of disappointing parents and friends is a common experience of children. They need our reassurance that Jesus is always with them. With our help, our children will learn that it takes courage, persistence, and faith in God to do what is right, but that peace and joy will follow them along the "Conversion Road."

GET READY!

Think about those times when a family member or friend helped relieve your fears and helped bring balance and peace back to your life. Recall times when you have helped relieve your child's fears and anxieties.

GET SET!

Gather together crayons and drawing paper. Add to the prayer table a small baptismal candle, a glass bowl of holy water from the parish church, and a fern or small evergreen branch to use for sprinkling.

GO!

Focus attention on the stained-glass art and ask your child to describe it. *(Jesus blessing the children)* Light the candle, assign "Leader" and "Reader" parts, and pray the prayer on page 71 with your child.

Then, using the holy water and branch, bless your child, saying,

> May God bless you and keep you!
> May God let his smile shine upon you and be kind to you!
> May God bless you and give you peace!
> *(Based on Numbers 6:24–26)*

Pages 72 and 73

We Listen

Direct attention to the illustration on pages 72 and 73. Explain that Jesus is with his Apostles, encouraging them and giving them his peace.

Read the Scripture verses paraphrased under "Jesus Gives Us Peace." Recall that God, our Father, sent his Son, Jesus, to show us how to live. We show that we are disciples of Jesus when we follow his command to love God and one another.

Emphasize that the Father sends the Holy Spirit to help us obey Jesus' command. Jesus also gave the disciples the gift of his peace to help them in loving and forgiving others. Stress Jesus' message of peace in the last paragraph.

Activity

Introduce the activity on page 73 by asking your child to think about a time when he was afraid or troubled. Explain that we can pray to the Holy Spirit to guide us and give us the strength to follow Jesus' teachings. Invite your child to fill in the missing words to complete the prayer to the Holy Spirit.

Invite him to share his responses. *(first line: heart, life, home, days, world, or similar words; second line: life, love, joy, peace, or similar words; third line: Jesus)*

With My Family

Share this saying with your child: "Fear knocked at the door. Faith answered. And no one was there." Gaining trust and confidence as they grow helps most children overcome childhood fears, but we can also answer our fears with faith in the presence of the Holy Spirit.

Pages 74 and 75

We Learn

Read the title and the first paragraph under "Jesus Keeps Calling Us to Conversion" on page 74. Explain that when Jesus calls us to conversion, he asks us to turn away from sin and turn toward God. Jesus continually calls us to love God and one another. When we sin, it is important to seek God's forgiveness and begin again.

Then read the second paragraph. You may wish to review Jesus' Great Commandment and New Commandment, found on page 22 in your child's book.

Then read the third paragraph, emphasizing that the Holy Spirit reminds us of Jesus' teachings and guides us to do what is right.

Direct attention to the photos on page 74. Ask, "Why is the girl smiling?" *(Her sins are forgiven and she is full of peace.)*

Read the first and second paragraphs under "Celebrating the Sacrament" on page 75. Emphasize that through the ministry of the priest, God frees us from sin and gives us new life. Explain the meaning of "Alleluia."

Then read the last paragraph. Remind your child that we should do our penance as soon as possible after receiving the Sacrament. Have your child recall that a penance may be saying a prayer or doing a kind act. After the priest dismisses us, we can remain in church for quiet prayer. We can ask the Holy Spirit to help us do our penance.

42 *Celebrate and Remember: Reconciliation* Home Guide

Activity

Read the directions for the activity and review absolution with your child. For the drawing, brainstorm words for the way he might feel. *(happy, peaceful, joyful, etc.)* Explain that this drawing does not have to look real. It can be a beautiful combination of joyful, happy, or peaceful colors. Remind your child to write "Alleluia!" under the drawing.

••••••••••••••••• Pages 76 and 77 •••••••••••••••

We Learn

Read together the first paragraph of "We Are Easter People." Explain that Easter is the day Jesus rose from the dead and gave us new life.

Then read the second paragraph. Our Baptism day is important because it is the day we were given new life and we became Easter people.

Continue by reading the paragraph on page 77. Remind your child that in the Sacrament of Reconciliation, we are given more new life. Ask, "What are some ways we can share the new life of Jesus with others?" *(by doing something good for someone, saying something kind, or being a friend to someone who is sad)* Encourage your child to suggest other ways we share God's life.

Activity

Read together the activity directions, and explain them to your child. After he has circled his word, invite him to draw a symbol or picture to show this word. Explain that a *symbol* is a picture that reminds us of something important.

Faith Highlights

Read the Golden Rule from Matthew 7:12. Recall with your child some kind acts people have done for him and others, and encourage him to treat others in the same way. Explain the difference between "getting even" with someone and treating someone the way we would *like* to be treated ourselves. What is Jesus telling us to do?

With My Family

Follow the directions for the "Name That Disciple" game. Design a certificate that you can duplicate and that recognizes each individual's best contribution. After the name of the family member, you can print, "who is excellent at ____." Hand out the certificates to be featured on the wall or desk of the individual family member's room.

Additional Activity

▸ Explain the notion of a *peaceable kingdom* to your child as a place where everyone honors the dignity of all and tries to be of service. Consider what it would mean at home, in school, or in your neighborhood if everyone tried to make that place a peaceable kingdom. Talk about concrete examples. Then ask your child to draw people in action in one of these places, living in peace and harmony with one another. Pray to the Holy Spirit for the courage to be peacemakers.

······· Pages 78 and 79 ·······

 ## We Live

Read together the Heart to Heart paragraph. Remind your child that Jesus is always with us, even though we cannot see him. Explain that Jesus is always happy to meet us in the Sacrament of Penance and Reconciliation, and that this Sacrament helps us to follow him more closely. We can meet Jesus in this Sacrament all during our lives!

Activity

Read together the directions for the Conversion Road activity. Challenge your child to choose ideas that will help him to be a faithful disciple of Jesus and to write them on the stepping-stones. Conclude by reminding him that every day Jesus calls us to conversion through loving God and loving and helping one another.

Saint Spotlight

Read together the paragraph about Saint Francis of Assisi. Talk about Saint Francis and ways he shared God's love and peace with others. In those days, sometimes cities went into battle with other cities. Saint Francis convinced the leaders to stop fighting and to live in peace.

With My Family

Teach the Peace Prayer (on page 93 in the child's book) to your family. Say it as a grace before meals for a week so that it will become familiar.

Additional Activity

▶ Review with your child what he has learned during this preparation program. Go back through the eight chapters and, using the Scripture illustrations and photos, ask him to tell you in his own words what he learned in each chapter. Gently correct any misunderstandings.

Then ask whether he feels ready to receive the Sacrament. Answer any questions he may have. Encourage him to print out those things he wants to remember on the day of his First Reconciliation.

Reviewing the Lesson

Help your child to recall the key points learned in this lesson:

- The Holy Spirit has been sent to us to help us follow Jesus.
- In the Sacrament of Reconciliation, we are freed from our sins and we go in peace. Then we do our penance as soon as possible.
- We are Easter people! Alleluia!

······· Page 80 ·······

 ## We Pray

Draw attention to the photo of the Paschal candle. Elicit from your child that the candle is the tall Easter candle that we see in church, usually near the baptismal font. Remind him that *alleluia* is a happy word of praise that we sing, especially during the Easter season (from the Easter Vigil to Pentecost Sunday). Assign "Reader" parts for the prayer. Then light the candle, take the part of "Leader," and pray the prayer with your child.

Acknowledgments

The scriptural quotations on page 21 are from the *New American Bible with Revised New Testament and Revised Psalms.* Copyright © 1991, 1986, and 1970 by the Confraternity of Christian Doctrine, Washington, D.C. Used by the permission of the copyright owner. All Rights Reserved. No part of the *New American Bible* may be reproduced in any form without permission in writing from the copyright owner.

The words from the Mass on page 26 are from *The Roman Missal* © 2010, International Commission on English in the Liturgy (ICEL). English translation prepared by the ICEL.

During this book's preparation, all citations, facts, figures, names, addresses, telephone numbers, Internet URLs, and other pieces of information cited within were verified for accuracy. The authors and Saint Mary's Press staff have made every attempt to reference current and valid sources, but we cannot guarantee the content of any source, and we are not responsible for any changes that may have occurred since our verification. If you find an error in, or have a question or concern about, any of the information or sources listed within, please contact Saint Mary's Press.